Little People of the Earth

Ceramic Figures from Ancient America

Denver Art Museum
June 23, 1990 - January 27, 1991

This catalog has been supported by gifts from Ambassador Holland H. Coors and the Nova Albion Foundation. The exhibition it accompanies has been made possible by a gift from Ambassador Coors and a grant from the Colorado Council on the Arts and Humanities.

Cover: Three Chupícuaro-style figures, 300-100 BC *(25)*

Editor: Marlene Chambers
Designer: Mary H. Junda
Photographer: William O'Connor

Library of Congress Catalog Card Number: 90-81361
Printed in the United States of America
ISBN 0-914738-40-2

Published by the Denver Art Museum
100 West 14th Avenue Parkway
Denver, Colorado 80204

Little People of the Earth is dedicated with love and admiration to our esteemed First Lady Barbara Bush. Her manifest concern for family values and human needs is a guiding inspiration to all of us.

Holland H. Coors
Ambassador for the National Year
of the Americas

FOREWORD

Over the past quarter century, the Denver Art Museum has built an extraordinary collection of pre-Columbian art. Initially fostered by former director Otto K. Bach, this commitment has been strengthened by Bob Stroessner, the museum's first and only curator of New World art. Bob's enthusiasm and knowledge have attracted a group of dedicated collectors and supporters in the Colorado area. The 51 "families" of Little People selected for this special exhibition offer a rich cross-section of pre-Columbian cultures. Though they vary in style and sophistication, they all share a formal sculptural quality that ranks them as true works of art. Too often their charms are overlooked when they are ranged among larger stone and ceramic achievements from the New World.

For the opportunity to bring them to light in this exhibition, we are indebted especially to Ambassador Holland H. Coors, whose support of pre-Columbian projects has often been demonstrated, to the Nova Albion Foundation, which has also contributed important objects to the collection, and to the Colorado Council on the Arts and Humanities. Stroessner's efforts in organizing the exhibition have been matched only by the long-standing, generous support of Frederick Mayer, chairman of the museum board, and his wife Jan, who share a passionate commitment to pre-Columbian art.

We also owe a debt of acknowledgment to Professor Gillett Griffin of Princeton University for his intelligent introduction to the catalog and a special thanks to Teddy Dewalt, whose volunteer assistance was invaluable to Bob Stroessner at every level of exhibition organization and catalog writing. Jeremy Hillhouse and G. F. Lauder deserve to be singled out for their ingenious and beautiful installation of the exhibition. The sensitive color photography in the catalog was the work of Bill O'Connor, while the handsome design was done by Mary Junda. A particular acknowledgment must be made to Marlene Chambers for the editorial expertise she brought to the project that has touched all aspects of the exhibition and its catalog.

Lewis Inman Sharp, Director
Denver Art Museum

AMERICA'S FUGITIVE FIGURINES

The key to the enigma of man's emergence as artist lies buried under countless veneers of evolutionary change. The wonder of it is that man is the only animal capable of creating images that can be "read" thousands of years later. This uniquely human characteristic was dramatically demonstrated in 1879 when a twelve-year-old girl pointed out to her father marks she could read as animals on the ceiling of a cave in Altamira, Spain. The late Stone-Age origin of these majestic paintings of bison was not accepted until 1902, but since then we have become increasingly aware of the extraordinary beauty and prodigious antiquity of our visual patrimony and the artistic importance of archaeological finds.

Man's earliest artistic efforts may have been inspired by the desire to enhance and decorate his own body by painting, tattooing, scarification, and head deformation. Animism and shamanism must later have moved him to depict animals that were vitally important to his life. About the same time, he also began to create effigies of the human figure.

An overwhelming number of ancient human images show the female form. These are generally read as "fertility" figures, haunting icons from the remote antiquity of the last Ice Age that rivet us with their impressive stylization. From the stone "Venus of Willendorf" (about 26,000 BC) to baked clay goddesses (about 6000 BC) found at Çatal Hüyük and Haçilar, two of the world's first cities, and Hittite and Indus Valley carvings (2000-1000 BC)—all are abstracted and conventionalized. Whether they appeared before or at the same time as the advent of great official religions, all exist outside their influence. It is fascinating that these tokens of man's earliest religious strivings seem to show a natural evolution that was repeated in a variety of cultures the world over.

The archaic Great Mother was eventually replaced by other gods—often male, sometimes of an awesome, warlike, or frightening nature. Emerging civilizations rallied around these official gods, constructing for them elaborate rituals, great temples, and political priesthoods. For these new gods, war and conquest were religious imperatives. In sophisticated ancient civilizations, official religions represented the ambitions of the elite, and images began to be placed in tombs as surrogate servants, entertainers, and guardians to provide the august dead with the same pleasures they had enjoyed in life. In ancient China, for instance, following the Qin dynasty (221-206 BC), elegant ceramic models of horses were interred with the elite to bring pleasure forever.

"Peasant" populations, on the other hand, were reactionary and more deeply rooted in traditions that touched their lives. They created and maintained their own folk traditions, somewhat akin to shamanism, and produced, in miniature, images that reflect their basic needs.

The earliest figurines were made of stone and bone, materials difficult to shape with primitive tools. The advent of ceramics brought new possibilities of form and expression. Discovering a brick-hard hearth under the ashes of fires built on clay floors may have first opened the human mind to clay as an adaptable and durable material. Reliefs sculpted on the clay floor of Le Tuc d'Audoubert cave in France suggest as much. These images of bison must have played a part in some shamanic hunting ritual about 15,000 BC. But the oldest sophisticated, highly burnished, independent ceramic figures in the ancient world come from Çatal Hüyük, Turkey (about 6000 BC), site of the earliest known religious shrines.

Ceramic technology was reinvented in a number of cultures the world over. In the New World, some of the earliest ceramics so far found are from Valdivia, on the southern coast of Ecuador. At Valdivia, as at most formative ceramic sites, pottery forms copy containers, such as gourds and stone bowls, already in use by the agricultural populace. But in Valdivia there were also terracotta figurines, mostly female, and a few stone votive figures of a more geometric nature. These clay ancestors are hauntingly powerful in spite of their diminutive size. They seem to wear wigs, like Egyptian wigs, and are generally nude. Are they companions, ancestors, or guides? We have no way of telling. But as our first American ceramic art they hold a particularly special place for me.

It is curious that not all developing cultures made figurines. None of the great Peruvian civilizations, for instance, featured small, solid, female figures. Attention turned to hollow vessels that could contain liquids or grains, and artists decorated these with extraordinary energy—sometimes painting their surfaces, but often shaping them as sculptures that relate to the mythology or the daily life of the people. Rarely do we find independent effigies, but when we do they resemble our dolls, rather than generic fertility figurines.

In South America, only Ecuador and Colombia place the same emphasis on clay figurines that we find in Mesoamerica. Ecuadorian figurines, especially, share some characteristics with those from Veracruz, Mexico. It is curious that the earliest deities of Mesoamerica are based on the same jungle animals as those that first appear in Ecuador and later in Peru's great primal civilization—Chavín.

In ancient Mesoamerica, we can see the first stirrings of organized religion in the sculpture of the Olmecs, with their rather awesome, stylized dragons and cleft-headed deities. Before and during the Olmec period and at the time of the great civilizations that followed the Olmec, the "peasant" cultures that surrounded and often supported their elite neighbors produced great quantities of figurines that reflect more conservative beliefs. Most of these little "folk" figurines are charmingly alive—far removed from frozen depictions of official deities. Generally found buried with the dead under the floors of their homes, these small works of art may have been intended as companions in the underworld.

The figurines of Mesoamerica stand out among those of other ancient cultures for their variety and sculptural beauty. They have an immediate appeal wanting elsewhere. A large poster created for the 1968 Olympics in Mexico shows a photograph of a sea of these figurine head fragments representing an international audience for the games. The variety of types and styles is remarkable. From all over Mesoamerica, they date from pre-Olmec to one fugitive head from the colonial period, a span of about 3,000 years.

Most of these figurines from Mesoamerica come to us without archaeological context—ghosts from the past turned up by farmers, road excavators, and brickyard workers. Figurines from San Jerónimo, for instance, were picked up by villagers and passing motorists from the debris of mounds leveled by bulldozers and road crews constructing the highway from Acapulco to Zihuatenejo along the Costa Grande of Guerrero. The legion of tiny fancy ladies from Chupícuaro were hastily salvaged by local farmers, collectors, and archaeologists from the rising waters of a great hydro-electric dam that submerged a number of ancient sites under a huge new lake.

But the most compelling "Venus" figurines in the world, called "pretty ladies" by archaeologists and collectors enchanted by their beauty, come from the site of a clay pit in the tiny village of Tlatilco on the northwestern outskirts of Mexico City. Here the growing city found a rich source of building brick below the pilgrimage shrine on top of the Cerro los Remedios, near the modern industrial area of Naucalpán. The deep deposits of clay had one flaw: the upper layers were full of human bones, ceramic vessels, jade beads, and thousands of figurines that had to be removed before the bricks were formed and fired. The first brick operations started in 1935, and word eventually spread among collectors of antiquities. One of the collectors, Miguel Covarrubias, was also an archaeologist and anthropologist. By 1942 he had managed to convince the Instituto Nacional de Antropología e Historia to dig some exploratory trenches.

More official archaeological digs followed in 1947, 1951, and on up to 1967. But archaeologists and collectors shared without malice in the salvage from Tlatilco. A newly arrived European emigrant (now a good friend of mine) heard Covarrubias give a public talk on Tlatilco in the mid-1940s. Deeply moved, he asked Covarrubias where the site was located. Covarrubias refused to tell him. Knowing that the original village had been situated on the shore of the ancient lake of Mexico, my friend traced the old shoreline until he found the site. Thereafter, he and Covarrubias went out every Saturday to buy pieces. Those Covarrubias collected now form a substantial part of the Olmec section of the Museo Nacional de Antropología, and my friend's collection is registered and will also become part of the nation's patrimony.

Another enthusiastic collector was a boy of twelve in 1944, sojourning in Mexico with his mother and brother. Thrilled to discover the archaeology of Mexico, he began to collect whatever he could as a hobby. After the artist Wolfgang Paalen introduced him to Tlatilco, he went there often, even though it took hours each way by bus. Because he was an enthusiastic kid who spoke Spanish and obviously had little money to spend, he could usually strike a better bargain than adult collectors or dealers.

One day at the brickworks, he and a school friend came upon workers digging out a burial in a new clay pit. The workers cared nothing for the contents of the burial, which included a great number of what appeared to be round clay pellets they disparagingly called "canicas." When the boy discovered a blue-green Olmec jade bead beneath the clay crust of one of these "marbles," he persuaded the men to slow down enough for the boys to scramble through each shovelful for "marbles." The young collectors left with 806 Olmec beads, priced at two for five centavos—the biggest cache of jade found in the Valley of Mexico up to that time and the largest jade necklace yet discovered in the Americas. No one can ever know how many beads escaped to be made into bricks or lost forever that day! It was collectors like these, as much as archaeologists, who salvaged what they could of the 4,000-year-old remains of a fascinating village.

Though Tlatilco yielded a bewildering number of figurine types, the "pretty ladies" remain the most beguiling. Averaging about three inches tall, they usually have rudimentary stumps for arms, bulbous hips that swell out from tiny waists and taper into cone-shaped legs, and charming adolescent faces surmounted by crisply filleted individual hairdos. Usually nude, some show body paint. Nipples and navels are deliciously picked out, and most of the ladies are smiling. They comprise a refreshing harem of happy, fertile, and eager adolescent girls. Like the courtesans of "primitive" Japanese prints, they first appear to be all alike and later emerge as individuals with distinct personalities.

These elegant, delicately crafted little ladies reflect centuries of abstraction and refinement. They did not suddenly materialize at Tlatilco. Their stylistic ancestors and relatives—removed in time and space—may be traced to the Mexican states of Morelos, Puebla, and Guerrero, and even to the countries of El Salvador and Honduras. But the quintessence of all "peasant" figurines in the world are those "pretty ladies" from Tlatilco. Alas! the site of Tlatilco is gone forever. The old brick quarry and the archaeological trenches are buried now under an endless sea of middle-class housing and marked only by a small regional museum.

Thus far we have been considering figurines that belong, more or less, to the "Venus" or "fertility" type. These are frontal, symmetrical, and stylized. But there are a great number of other figures—some small and solid, others larger and hollow—that have a place in our discussion.

The figures and figurines of West Mexico, created about 2,000 years ago (1,000 years after those of Tlatilco), depart severely from those we have already discussed. Ceramic sculpture from Colima, for instance, is comprised of both small solid figurines and larger hollow figures. We first notice that these figurines depict people caught up in activities. If they are men, they bear shields, brandish war clubs, or beat drums; if they are women, they grind corn, nurse, or carry babies. These were all created as tomb furniture. The larger burnished vessels provide for the needs of the eternal afterlife: tomb guardians; shamans to help guide and protect in the underworld; dogs, fowl, gourds, and peyote for food and sustenance. In Nayarit one even finds homes depicted—ideal homes being shared by families or whole village scenes. To us these resemble "folk art" and have been relegated to that status by some art historians. Functional and meaningful to those who made them, they bring us a refreshing glimpse of everyday life.

We have been discussing the art of the little people—"peasant" art. But the great civilizations also made figures in a different tradition. In addition to their formal ceremonial art, the Olmec produced a number of ceramic figurines—often covered with a fine, burnished, white kaolin slip, with touches of red and black pigment to pick out hair and certain features. These are generally removed from the abstractions of the "peasant" figurines produced at the same time. Stylized into ideal Olmec types, they probably stood for an elite group of those who felt themselves superior by bloodline to the "peasant" population. Even so, the figurines may have served the same function in the grave.

A number of great "Classic" cultures grew out of the surviving memory of Olmec civilization. The most enigmatic of these is Teotihuacán. It crystalized the first great Mesoamerican city plan and excites wonder today for its vast and dynamic space. It seems not to have had rulers or dynasties for the greater part of its existence. Perhaps it was built as the place where the gods of all Mesoamerica dwelled. If so, its populace may have been made up of barrios of different peoples who lived there in a seemingly egalitarian setting to be near celestial paradise. In any case, they left behind thousands of little figurines that record their clothing and fashions. One common type of figure, created apparently to dance eternally in the flowery paradise, is nothing but a little clay armature surmounted by a mold-made head. Since its limbs were jointed at the torso, the figure was probably intended to be dressed in fabric like a doll and may have held flower blossoms in its hands. Outside of these "dancers," most Teotihuacán figurines are static. The earliest were handmade and therefore somewhat lively. Later, the use of mold-made heads and then complete figures brought a classicism, but finally a dullness, to the ceramic production of Teotihuacán.

The iconography of Central Veracruz greatly influenced Teotihuacán; yet, its figurines are very different. Veracruz figures are generally larger, much more plastic, and seemingly happy. This is evident in the charming figures of El Faisán—especially the exuberant couples sitting on swings, enjoying themselves like children. But the figures that seem to typify the style of Central Veracruz are often called Remojadas, after a small village south of the city of Veracruz. Their trademark is a winning smile—one of the earliest true smiles in all of the history of art. The smile can vary from a smirk to a belly laugh. Recently, art historians have spoiled the innocence of these smiles by suggesting that these little folk are intoxicated or drugged to prepare them for a sacrificial death that will propel them into the eternal flowery paradise.

The Zapotecs of Oaxaca are credited with the invention of America's earliest writing system, as well as the corbel arch. Their great mountain-top acropolis of Monte Albán preceded the city of Teotihuacán by hundreds of years. But the Zapotecs avoided the use of figurines in the Classic period and instead provided their tombs with symbolic urns.

The Classic Maya, generally agreed to be the greatest of all ancient American civilizations, did create figurines for burial use, though their function is not very well understood. In Palenque, fragments of figurines are found smashed behind the forest temples, rather than in tombs. In Lagartero, which straddles the Chiapas/Guatemala border, elaborately molded figurines are found in ancient dumps.

But the most celebrated Maya figurines are found on Jaina, an island necropolis off the coast of the Yucatán. The figurines may have been brought there from many manufacturing places for burial with the dead, who had also been transported from the mainland. The figurines from Jaina are justly celebrated. They are both mold made and hand modeled and represent a variety of subjects—from victims of torture and scenes of autosacrifice to ideal male and female underworld companions and gods and goddesses. The nobility of some of the hand-modeled figures and the sense of humor of others, together with their naturalistic postures and near-portraiture, make them more accessible to our sensibilities today than most other ceramic figures from the ancient New World.

This, then, is a brief survey of the fugitive figurines, which were made long ago to accompany the dead. They derive from a series of cultures very foreign to ours. But, as examples of the very personal funerary possessions of our American cultural ancestors, they may help bring us closer to our forgotten past.

Gillett G. Griffin
Faculty Curator of Pre-Columbian and Primitive Art
The Art Museum, Princeton University

LITTLE PEOPLE OF THE EARTH

Never a man to let his enthusiasms be dampened by theory or conventional preconceptions, Albrect Dürer was overwhelmed by his first sight of plunder from the New World. Calling the Aztec treasures he saw in Antwerp "more beautiful to behold than miracles," Dürer could only marvel "at the subtle *ingenia* of people in far-off lands." This was extravagant praise from the first northern European artist to embrace the realist esthetic of Renaissance Italy, for none of the Mesoamerican objects that "gladdened . . . [his] heart" came even close to being a faithful copy of nature. Dürer's homage to an alien esthetic was all the more remarkable because he himself wrote theoretical treatises that helped spread and entrench the Renaissance values that still color the way we look at art: "The more accurately one approaches nature by way of imitation, the better and more artistic your work becomes."

The strong grip of Renaissance esthetics on Western consciousness has begun to weaken only in the last century. Lacking the eclectic appetite of Dürer, many of us even now find it difficult to appreciate the visual achievements of other cultural traditions. The classical image of man that dominated Western art for four centuries remains our yardstick for making value judgments. So it was that early scholars of pre-Hispanic American art found no more appropriate term than "classic" to describe the periods of cultural florescence in ancient America. The designation has been largely abandoned today because it is too broad to be useful, and many ethnologists have questioned its appropriateness. But our Western eyes are conditioned to appreciate most readily whatever is most flatteringly lifelike. We stand in awe before "classical" Maya figures *(47)* and find ourselves dismissing as "primitive" or "awkward" other pre-Columbian ceramic figurines that don't fit our Renaissance ideal *(12* or *24,* for example*)*. Although we can easily see a family resemblance among objects from the same place and time, it is sometimes difficult to accept their common distortions of the human figure as the intentional result of a set of values different from our own.

Yet, once we abandon ourselves to these wonderfully varied interpretations of the human form, we can begin to appreciate their achievement. They show the infinite scope of the human imagination, as well as the shared qualities people of all cultures have used to define their humanity. Although we really know very little about these ceramic images, we recognize in them characteristics of people we know. While their purpose remains a matter of scholarly speculation, their personalities speak to us across the centuries.

This exhibition presents a selection of small ceramic human figures in the Denver Art Museum's New World collection. For the first time, figurines from most of the major pre-Columbian cultures are shown together in a panorama that encourages comparative study and appreciation. Most of them were unearthed from burial sites, though some were found in ancient trash heaps. They are arranged here in "families" of stylistically similar figures, but only rarely did these groups originate in the same cache. Many of them are the products of village cultures, though some come from the great sophisticated theocracies that flourished for a time and then withered.

The earliest ceramic sculptures yet found in the New World come from sites near the small village of Valdivia in Ecuador (1). Tooth-shaped images of the human form carved from soft stone have been found in the deepest strata of these sites. Later strata give evidence that experiments with solid ceramic versions of these stone sculptures began about the same time as ceramic vessels first appeared (3500 BC). Successive archaeological layers (until about 2000 BC) tell a story of the development of increasingly defined details that make these images read more readily as human figures.

Almost nothing is known of the meaning or purpose of these small images. Although many scholars believe they are fertility figures, sex characteristics are not emphasized as they usually are in such cases. Fashioned from a single coil of clay, the figure was made by bending a coil over against itself, like a clothespin, with the ends forming legs and the rounded bend at top serving for a head. Fusing the sides beneath the bend created the torso, and a little pinching and pulling gave the form more definition, with details incised by a sharp tool. These figures are fully rounded and their backs as carefully finished as the fronts. As ceramic technology developed, surfaces were burnished, slips of pastelike clay painted on before firing, and pellets of clay applied to give the figures more detail. However, since large solid objects explode during firing, Valdivia figurines always remained small, apparently because the idea of hollow-figure construction didn't occur to their makers.

A major technical development occurred with the Chorrera hollow figures (1500-500 BC) found over an extensive area of Ecuador (3). Because they are effigy vessels, these figures suggest that the revolutionary idea for hollow ceramic sculpture originated in the practice of embellishing containers with sculptural details. The thinness of the clay walls, highly burnished colored slips, and smooth, evenly rounded forms proclaim the technical mastery of Chorrera potters. Early Guangala (500 BC-AD 100) solid figures found along coastal Ecuador are considerably flatter in conception than Valdivia figures (1,2), and Late Guangala hollow figures (500 BC-AD 100) made possible by Chorrera technical advances retain this penchant for frontality, though they are necessarily more fully three-dimensional (4).

The hand-made figural tradition continued throughout South America until about AD 500, when press molds radically changed ceramic production. The seams visible along the sides of the Jama-Coaque figures from Ecuador (6) and the Mochica examples from north-coast Peru (10) show where finely detailed press-mold façades were joined to the plain clay slabs that form their backs. Made by master artists, the molds allowed mass production and discouraged original expression and experimentation. Hand-modeled examples from highland Carchi represent the end of the sculptural tradition in pre-Columbian Ecuador (7). Although stiff and awkward in their poses, they achieve a degree of naturalism not suggested by their abstract and stylized predecessors. Sun-dried or fired at very low temperatures, Carchi figures didn't always survive their damp burial in deep shaft tombs but sometimes partially dissolved like adobe.

Small solid human figures appeared only briefly in Peru. They were soon displaced by the hollow effigy vessel concept and given the stirrup-spout that characterizes Peruvian ceramics of the next 1,000 years. The cylindrical Chavín-style ocarina (8) and the even more abstract Paracas or Proto-Nazca figure (9) included here are so minimally modeled they show little promise of the flowering of a realistic modeling tradition that was to follow in Mochica ceramics (10).

Although little is known about its formative stages, scholars generally identify the Olmec as the "mother culture" of Mesoamerica, an area that includes present-day Mexico and its neighbors south to Nicaragua. Since no developmental period for Olmec ceramics has been found in the Olmec heartland of

Veracruz and Tabasco in coastal Mexico, Carlo Gay and Gillett Griffin have proposed an origin in the Guerrero highlands, where an extraordinary figurine complex was unearthed near Xochipala. Remarkable for their lifelike postures and naturalistically modeled bodies, these figures so accurately suggest the human skeletal structure beneath muscled flesh that they were first rejected as forgeries when large numbers of them began appearing in the 1960s. Continued research and testing has established their date at about 1500 BC, and some of the solid figures seem to offer the earliest examples of anecdotal ceramic groupings in Mesoamerica. The attention given to individual personalities in these early Xochipala examples gives way to increasing stylization in middle and late period figures.

Other nearby sites have yielded ceramic figures related to those found at Xochipala. At Xalitla, Guerrero, for instance, several hundred small figures reportedly turned up in a single meter of earth displaced while digging a well. Their profusion of attitudes and clothing styles suggests interacting groups that might represent an entire village (14b-d). Batlike staffs, wrappings around arms and legs, or large rings and pads on hands and knees may represent ball-game regalia. Thermoluminescence tests have verified dates of about 1000 BC for the Xalitla figures.

Las Bocas, in the state of Puebla, Mexico, is another important highland Olmec site, long noted for the artistic and technical achievement of its naturalistic figurines. Made from an unusually fine clay and covered with a creamy-white slip, these figures were highly burnished and overpainted with red and black glyphlike designs after firing. Though tiny, the example we've included in our Olmec group (14a) conveys an animated monumentality reminiscent of the famous Olmec stone wrestler. A large female figure (16), whether from Las Bocas, Tlatilco, or one of a number of sites along the Cuautla River in Morelos, shows a shift to refined stylization. Sharp cuts inside the elbow joint, at the back of the knees, and at the buttocks ally this figure to a less elegant example from the Valley of Mexico (17a) and identify them both as a rare type found at a number of highland sites.

Another highland Guerrero site now being excavated, Teopantecuanitlán, may prove to be an important early Olmec center, the first to be discovered in the highlands with monumental public sculpture, ceremonial architecture, and a complex drainage system. Our ceramic figures from the

Teopantecuanitlán region*(15)*, like most figures from village cultures in the Valley of Mexico, make no attempt to represent the human form accurately, but follow a local tradition that conveys the concept of humanness in a simplified abstraction.

Among the Valley of Mexico sites, Tlatilco is probably the best known. Here, near Mexico City, workers digging clay for bricks unearthed hundreds of ancient burials in the 1940s and 1950s. No other New World site has offered such a delightful profusion of styles and figure types. Some examples found here show the influence of sophisticated Las Bocas models *(14e-f)*; others illustrate a bewildering variety of local village styles *(17)*. The overwhelming majority of Tlatilco figures represent females of the type dubbed "pretty lady" by collectors and scholars charmed by their frankly inviting characteristics *(17f-h)*. Even when they are completely nude, their elaborate and highly individualistic coiffures give these figures the appearance of being "dressed to the nines" for some special occasion, and their stubby arms are thrown open in a welcoming gesture. All are relatively flat, frontal, and symmetrical, and, although most appear to be standing on tiptoe, they cannot, in fact, stand alone. The few male figures found at Tlatilco and nearby Tlapacoya generally wear distinctive costumes that suggest a ceremonial or official role *(17c)*. Double-headed or double-faced figures that may represent ancient concepts of duality or transformation occur with some frequency at Tlatilco and other sites in the Valley of Mexico *(18)*.

The Olmec seem to have developed from small isolated villages to great ceremonial complexes and expanded their sphere of influence from Mexico to present-day Costa Rica within a relatively short time. A large family of Olmec-derived styles, little studied as yet, comes from the Pacific coast of Honduras and El Salvador *(20)*. Stiffly frontal female figures *(22)* and fleshy, seated or reclining Olmec types *(20a-b)* seem related to an assortment of stone monoliths that must have served as monumental sculpture for ceremonial centers with perishable architecture that has disappeared without a trace. Because there has been little archaeological investigation of this region, current knowledge is scant and stylistic terminology inexact. We do know that most ceramic figures from this south Pacific area have been intentionally broken. Hollow effigy vessels, some with a Peruvianlike stirrup spout *(20b)*, have been found here, as well as a number of figures with distinctive, exaggerated shoulders similar to stone bench figures from the same region that are thought to portray an ancestor or mythic founder of the tribe *(21)*. The concave chests and backs of figures from Chalchuapa suggest that the heads were modeled separately and attached by pushing enough clay upward from back and front to build a neck column to receive them *(21,22)*. An assembly-line production that allowed the best potters to concentrate on heads, which assistants later attached to trunks, has been postulated to explain why so many of these figures are found broken at the necks: if the heads were dry at the time of attachment, the weakness of the joint would be subject to such fracture. Kaminaljuyú, the most important ancient urban center in highland Guatemala, is unfortunately buried under modern Guatemala City, where archaeological excavation is impractical and accidental finds infrequent. The little evidence available indicates that local ceramic production included both hollow and solid figures whose fat, nearly neckless bodies recall the Olmec seated "baby" ceramic type *(23)*.

From the coastal region near Acapulco come distinctive San Jerónimo figures *(24)*, easily recognizable by their relatively large, elongated heads and short bodies, as well as the deep punctuation and incising used to define details of their ornate clothing, coiffures, and headgear. In their frontality they resemble the widely distributed Chupícuaro-style figures of the same period from Guanajuato *(25-28)*. But the Chupícuaro figures are more volumetric, somewhat more restrained in their decorative elaboration, and much more varied in figure type. Local village variants on the Chupícuaro model probably reflect local fashions in beauty, hairstyle, and jewelry that served as emblems of tribal identity *(27)*. The Chupícuaro style also inspired figures from nearby Michoacán *(29)*, where attention again shifts away from the figure itself to decorative effects.

The extensive shaft-tomb complex of West Coast Mexico has yielded three major ceramic styles named for the modern states in which the tombs appear: a southern style (Colima), a central or inland style (Jalisco), and a northern style (Nayarit). Small tomb figures from all three areas are generally free-standing and fully rounded so they can interact anecdotally. The sculptor's interest centers on depicting appropriate body gestures, and forms are simplified to essential volumes and the few props or clothing elements necessary to signify roles *(30-32)*. Because naturalistic representation of the body's articulation is less important than fluid body movements, these figures appear jointless, as if they were made of rubber *(34)*. One of the most interesting anecdotal ceramic types comes from the Nayarit of Ixtlán del Río, who constructed elaborate vignettes set in temples, ballcourts, and houses *(38)*. Made of slabs and coils of clay built on flat clay platforms, these models depict a host of perishable objects—architecture, textiles, basketry—for which we have no other record.

The great urban theocracies of pre-Columbian Mesoamerica, like the village cultures they arose out of and dominated, produced small ceramic figures, as well as monumental stone architecture and sculpture. Probably the largest of these city-states was Teotihuacán, "Place of the Gods," which was rebuilt five or six times during its long history. The city, with perhaps a quarter of a million inhabitants at its height, radiated out for miles along the northern edge of the Valley of Mexico. Archaeological excavations have concentrated on the vast ceremonial precinct, where no burials have been found, but broken ceramic figures by the thousands have emerged from the mounds of rubble used as core material for successive building programs. Of the twenty-some figural styles unearthed at Teotihuacán, only a few are represented here. They reveal a technical progression from early hand-made village styles *(39)*, through the first steps in mold development *(40a-b)*, to fully mass-produced press-mold examples *(40c-d)*. Even the earliest of these seem to reflect a greater attention to the insignia of ceremonial office than to the figure, which is often little more than a cursory mannequin. Ceramics from nearly all Mesoamerican sites of the period show the effects of Teotihuacán hegemony *(35,41)*.

The Maya ruling class appears to have established its legitimacy through marriage alliances with the rulers of Teotihuacán, and, because Maya centers rose in the humid south as Teotihuacán declined in the central highlands, the Maya actually seem heir to Teotihuacán wealth and power. Sometimes called the "Greeks of America," the Maya rival ancient Egypt, China, and Europe for their achievements in mathematics, astronomy, writing, and architecture. As represented in ceramic sculpture found concentrated in tombs on or near their Jaina Island necropolis, the Maya figural ideal is similar enough to Western Renaissance interpretations of Greek and Roman forms that it satisfies our own enduring classical standards of beauty. The anatomical proportions and well-observed physical attitudes of Jaina figures make them appear to our eyes as the most lifelike of pre-Columbian ceramic sculptures.

Yet, like the Greek sculpture we unconsciously compare them to, these figures are not realistic, but generalized and idealized.

Like Greek sculpture, too, they very probably represent gods and mythological heroes or deifications of priestly aristocrats rather than specific people, though scholars once thought they could be portraits. As in Teotihuacán figures, attributes of office often overwhelm the human form *(48)*. Elegantly carved aristocratic faces are frozen in an impassive stare that is frequently duplicated exactly by mold-made technology. Other figures, when they portray fantastic characters of mythology or are distorted for a functional purpose, are significantly more plastic, with more expressive faces *(46)*.

Jaina figures reflect the wealth and standing of the deceased in whose tomb they were placed. Early examples were entirely hand made, but the finest followed the Teotihuacán period III practice *(40a-b)* of topping hand-modeled bodies with mold-made heads *(47)*. The least expensive Jaina figures were completely press-molded like the group we've included from Honduras, the southern limits of Maya dominance *(49)*.

As the priestly caste grew in political power, the theocratic cultures of the New World reduced religious figures and concepts to abstract stylizations so far removed from their original subjects that they were probably indecipherable to all but initiates. Teotihuacán used small, easily transported press-mold flats of such glyphlike symbols to broadcast its visual vocabulary over long distances. In the stiffness and frontality of their treatment, as well as the extreme geometric abstraction of their costume elements, two small effigy urns from Monte Albán show the impact of this conventionalized and hermetic Teotihuacán style on the Zapotec of Oaxaca *(44)*.

In contrast, though it incorporated many Teotihuacán forms and motifs, the sculptural tradition of the Gulf Coast is less austere, sharp-angled, and volumetric than the art of central Mexico. It tends, instead, toward elegantly baroque curvilinear shapes, often elaborated through repetition. The decorative scroll designs that enliven the surface of the little whistle and rattle figures from the Upper Papaloapan River are typical *(43)*. The Huastec group from northern Veracruz represents yet another distinct sculptural style *(45)*. Local figural traditions prevailed even after Teotihuacán-style molds replaced the technique of hand modeling and appliquéing.

One of the treasures of the Denver Art Museum collection is a rare tomb group believed to have come from the Tehuantepec region *(50)*. Made after the collapse of the theocratic dynasties during a period dominated by militaristic city-states, this is one of the few groupings from the same burial that have survived separations wrought by lootings and haphazard accidental excavations. This "throne scene" resembles tableaus painted on late Maya vessels, but its visual style relates to both Veracruz and Monte Albán examples.

Although miniature ceramic figures continued to be made until the time of the Spanish Conquest, plastic expressiveness was sacrificed to the symbolic message ceaselessly repeated in figures cast from coarsely modeled flats (51). Early Spanish historians tell us that the Aztec used such figures to honor particular gods and that celebrations of one god or another occurred daily. Figures began to be made from wood, resin, straw, or even edible meal and seeds. These late votive offerings signal the end of an ancient and fascinating tradition.

Though our review of pre-Columbia America's myriad figural traditions, like the exhibition itself, is not intended to be exhaustive, it offers a glimpse of the infinite inventiveness of the human imagination. The variety and vitality of human nature speaks to us through these little figures, who transcend boundaries of time, language, and cultural differences to remind us of our common humanity.

Robert J. Stroessner
Curator of New World Art
Denver Art Museum

CATALOG

1
Ecuador, Valdivia
3500-2000 BC
Solid, hand-modeled, 2⅝ to 4⅞ in.
Archaeological sites near the small village of Valdivia have yielded ceramic figures like these, the earliest yet found in the New World. Their extreme simplification and toothlike features recall earlier stone carvings of the human form from the same area. This group includes (far left) a rare male figure with horned headdress.

2
Ecuador, Guangala
500 BC-AD 100
Solid, hand-modeled, ⅞ to 3¼ in.
The forked legs and long torsos of these examples of the early Guangala style show a similarity to the Valdivia model for the human form. However, the Guangala figures are flatter and have been given noses and triangular, projecting arms. Some of their features have been defined by applying shaped clay pellets to their surfaces. One of the earliest New World ceramics to show jewelry in use, the large center figure even wears a nose ornament. The geometric incising could represent body paint, scarification, or clothing.

3
Ecuador, Chorrera
1500-500 BC
Hollow, hand-modeled, 4 to 11½ in.
The technical mastery shown by Chorrera
hollow figures has earned them a reputation
as one of the high points in New World
ceramic production. But their esthetic appeal
rests on their elegant design with its perfect
symmetry, evenly swelling forms, and
rhythmically repeated curves. The engaged
arms and helmetlike treatment of hair or
headgear are typical of Chorrera figures.

4
Ecuador, Guangala
500 BC-AD 100
Hollow, hand-modeled, 7¾ in.
Late Guangala hollow figures like this were
made possible by Chorrera technical
advances (3). The refined proportions of its
cylindrical forms—headdress, arms, torso,
and legs—give the figure balance and
harmony. The restrained use of a surface
pattern of incised lines to accentuate three-
dimensional curves helps make this an
outstanding example of its kind.

5
Ecuador, Los Esteros
Bahía phase
500 BC-AD 100
Solid, hand-modeled, 3¼ to 4¾ in.
The human figure is portrayed here as a series of flat, simplified planes, whose curving outlines are perhaps intended to suggest volume. Among the few applied features are "coffee-bean" eyes and mouths and flat, beaklike noses. This group, a type found only in a series of beach-front caches near Los Esteros, illustrates one of a profusion of regional styles that developed in this period.

6
Ecuador, Jama-Coaque
Chone style
AD 200-600
Hollow, press-molded, 3½ to 10½ in.
The precision, uniform symmetry, and standardization of these figures give them away immediately as mass-produced, press-molded works. D-shaped eyes are an identifying characteristic of the rare Chone style.

7
Ecuador, Carchi
AD 1200-1400
Solid, hand-modeled, 7¾ and 6¼ in.
These low-fired figures represent the end of the figural tradition in Ecuador. Despite their stiff poses, they achieve a degree of realism in their full volumes and articulation of body parts. Apart from the eyes, facial features show an attempt to represent life-models accurately.

8
Peru, Tembladera
Chavín style
700-400 BC
Hollow, hand-modeled, 6¾ in.
This almost unarticulated cylinder relies on incised and painted surface details to represent the human figure. The feline headdress, facial markings, and conch-shell trumpet strapped to the shoulder suggest that the figure represents a god, a god-impersonator, or a shaman. Appropriately enough, the conch shell terminates at the back in a cylindrical mouthpiece that facilitates its function as an ocarina.

9
Peru, Paracas or Proto-Nazca
500-100 BC
Hollow, hand-modeled, 5⅞ in.
Well known for the quality of their hollow effigy vessels, Peruvian potters produced very few small hollow figurines like this. Even more determinedly cylindrical than the Tembladera ocarina (8), this rare figure has been given only minimal sculptural articulation to define its human features. The painted parallel lines emphasize its pronounced verticality and help give it a surprising monumentality for its size.

10
Peru, Mochica
AD 400-600
Hollow, press-molded, 2½ and 3⅛ in.
Since they are not intended as vessels, these diminutive figures lack the stirrup-spout usually associated with Mochica ceramics. But, even at their small size, they show the Mochica potter's sophisticated skill in depicting the human face: they combine a realism that suggests portraiture with the simplification and stylization typical of idealism. Like the Jama-Coaque figures (6), they're made of press-mold fronts seamed at the sides to a slab of plain clay. Their compact forms and regular, repeated curves give them a pleasing solidity and unity.

11
Colombia, Tairona
AD 1000-1500
Hollow, hand-modeled, 4¾ in.
A great deal of attention has been lavished on the accurate representation of this figure's clothing and actions. Although the feet and legs are still treated as a single column, like those of the much earlier hollow Guangala figure (4), the arms are now entirely disengaged. In spite of the static leg treatment, the backward slant of the thighs and forward bend of the torso at the waist give the figure the appearance of movement, as if he were dancing while accompanying himself with a mouth instrument and rattle. His apronlike skirt and feather bustle are reminiscent of New Mexican Kachina dance clothing; the elaborate tasseled turban helps disguise the whistle in the head.

12
Venezuela, Lake Maracaibo region
Timoto Cuica culture
AD 800-1200
Solid and hollow, hand-modeled
2¹⁄₁₆ to 4¼ in.
The fantastic characteristics of these little figures are generally even more exaggerated in female subjects, who are distinguished by the excessive width of their heads and their fat buttocks and thighs. The elongation and high placement of their applied "coffee-bean" eyes accentuate their froglike appearance. More than half of these examples show traces of paint in patterns of parallel lines.

13
Costa Rica
Cartago, Turrialba;
Guanacaste, Nicoya, Guabal style
AD 500-1100
Solid (except three large figures),
hand-modeled, 1⅜ to 6⅜ in.
Despite their swelling hips, the two female
figures on the left from highland Costa Rica
are much flatter in conception than the richly
colored and burnished figures from Nicoya,
with their exaggerated volumes.

14
Mexico
Puebla, Las Bocas;
Guerrero, Xalitla;
and Distrito Federal, Tlatilco
Olmec style
1500-1000 BC
Solid, hand-modeled, 2 to 5½ in.
The great variety of Olmec styles is illustrated
by this group: the figure from Las Bocas
seated at left is relatively realistic in its details
and facial expression; although stylized, the
three central figures (Xalitla) show a high
degree of individuation; the two seated figures
at right (Tlatilco) have been abstracted to a
generalized type.

15
Mexico, Guerrero
Teopantecuanitlán region
1500-1000 BC
Solid, hand-modeled, 3¼ and 4⅜ in.
These little figures, with their distinctive
"coffee-bean" eyes, "pretzel" arms, and
prominent eyebrows, come from a newly
identified Olmec area in the highlands.

16
Mexico, Puebla
Las Bocas ?
1300-800 BC
Solid, hand-modeled, 7 in.
Sensitive design decisions distinguish this figure from other examples of the "pretty lady" type (17f-h). Its low center of gravity and heavy volumes are lightened and uplifted by the long neck and tilted head, the upward thrust of the breasts, and the repeated, upturned angles of heel, groin, buttocks, and browridge. The delicately curving volumes of abdomen and thighs and the gentle slope that dissolves the distinction between shoulder and breast reveal the hand of a master.

17
Mexico, Distrito Federal
Tlatilco and Tlapacoya
1200-500 BC
Solid, hand-modeled, 1½ to 5¼ in.
These figures from the Valley of Mexico demonstrate a great variety of village styles. Their relatively small breasts, slim waists, wide hips, and open arms qualify the three female figures at right as "pretty lady" types. The difference in details that gives each a distinct personality is also characteristic of "pretty ladies." The group shown here includes an unusually large number of male figures since only ten percent of the figures unearthed at Tlatilco are male.

18
Mexico, Distrito Federal
Tlatilco
1200-500 BC
Solid, hand-modeled, 3⅛ to 4 in.
Two-headed female figures occur with some frequency in the Valley of Mexico. They may be visual expressions of ancient New World concepts of duality or transformation.

19
Mexico, Distrito Federal
Tlatilco
1200-500 BC
Solid, hand-modeled, 2½ and 3¼ in.
These small figures exemplify a late type (known as "K") characterized by "goggle" eyes, deep, cylindrical earplugs, beaklike noses, open mouths, and flipperlike hands and feet. Their repeated ovals create an appealing rhythmic harmony.

20
El Salvador, Chalchuapa
Honduras, Playa de los Muertos
Olmecoid style
1000-500 BC
Solid (except effigy vessel), hand-modeled 3 to 5½ in.
The Olmec style was dispersed as far south as the Pacific coastal regions of El Salvador and Honduras. This diverse group includes an example (far left) whose fleshy body type and seated, spread-leg pose quite closely relate to the Olmec "seated baby" type. The legs of the reclining effigy vessel next to it form a stirrup-spout.

21
El Salvador, Chalchuapa
600-350 BC
Solid, hand-modeled, 7 to 9 in.
These figures are characterized by exaggerated shoulders and a peculiar set of the head that emphasizes the flat planes of the face and makes the jaw jut forward pugnaciously. Their heavy hips and hollow-chested, thin upper torsos are Olmec traits. The nearly circular area enclosed by the shoulders and arms recalls the arm treatment in the little Olmec figures from Guerrero (15).

22
El Salvador, Chalchuapa
1000-600 BC
Solid, hand-modeled, 9 in.
The broad hips, shelflike shoulders, and thrusting jaw of this standing female figure identify her as an ancestor of other figures from this site (21). She also shares with them other family features derived from Olmec sources: caplike hair treatment, open mouth, and prominently defined teeth.

23
Guatemala, Kaminaljuyú
Olmecoid style
500-100 BC
Hollow (except figure at right), hand-modeled, 5 to 7 in.
Like other figures from this site, the seated, fat, almost neckless bodies of this group resemble the babylike figural ideal of Olmec sculpture while their heads are more naturalistically treated.

24
Mexico, Guerrero
Costa Grande area
San Jerónimo style
400-100 BC
Solid, hand-modeled, 3½ to 5 in.
Although these figures share some
characteristics with Chupicuaro examples
(25-27), their rectangular, relatively outsize
heads are distinctive. So flat they seem like
cut-out cookies, their surfaces are loaded
down with pinched, punched, applied, and
deeply incised decorative details. San
Jerónimo figures rarely appear nude, possibly
because clothing afforded more decorative
opportunities than the nude body.

25
Mexico, Guanajuato
Chupicuaro style
300-100 BC
Solid, hand-modeled, 2⅝ to 5½ in.
More restrained in decoration than their San
Jerónimo relatives (24), the widely distributed
Chupicuaro-style figures also show more
variety. In a rhythmic repetition of rounded
forms that includes even kneecaps, the little
figure at far left reflects another difference—
a greater interest in sculptural volume. In the
simplified, pendulous forms that define
breasts and belly, the central figure recalls the
famous stone Venus of Willendorf (25,000 BC).

26
Mexico, Guanajuato
Chupicuaro style
300-100 BC
Solid, hand-modeled, 1¼ to 4½ in.
The beaklike nose treatment, "coffee-bean"
eyes, and cockscomb headgear of these
figures suggest the wide variety of tribal
variations found in Chupicuaro ceramics.

27
Mexico, Guanajuato
Chupícuaro style
300-100 BC
Solid, hand-modeled, 3¼ and 3 in.
The thick necklaces worn by this diminutive couple probably signal a tribal costume and led to the name of "choker variant" for this type.

28
Mexico, Guanajuato
Chupícuaro style
Red slip variety
300-100 BC
Solid, hand-modeled, 2½ and 8½ in.
Large, hollow figures from Chupícuaro are finished in the same glossy red slip and cream and black geometric decorations of Chupícuaro ceramic vessels. These unusual solid examples appear to be wearing painted bloomers that recall those incised on the San Jerónimo figures (24). Their "diamond" eye shape is one of several variants found on figures of this type.

29
Mexico, Michoacán and Colima
200 BC-AD 200
Solid, hand-modeled, ⁵⁄₁₆ to 5¾ in.
Like the San Jerónimo examples (24), Michoacán figures are somewhat flatter and more decked out with detail than their Chupícuaro models (25-27). The two on the left have the two-hole "button" eye typical of figures from Cuitzéo, Michoacán, and the white-clay figure on the far right wears a remarkable featherwork collar. The rare sets of tiny beads shown here have punctures through the head at ear-level for threading.

30
Mexico, Colima
Archaic style
200 BC-AD 200
Solid, hand-modeled, 4¼ and 5 in.
Notable for their simplified, curving, almost jointless forms, small figures from Colima achieve an effect of lively, fluid movement. These two warriors, one with a sling, the other with club and shield, have the pointed nose and "doughnut" eyes typical of the archaic style.

31
Mexico, Colima
Archaic style
200 BC-AD 200
Solid, hand-modeled, 3¼ and 3 in.
Unlike many small ceramic figures from other areas of the New World, Colima figures were designed to stand unaided so they could be set up in narrative scenes. One of these musicians blows a conch-shell trumpet, the other plays a turtle-shell drum. Like the pair of warriors (30), the musicians were found together in the same burial. All four examples are whistles.

32
Mexico, Colima
Archaic style
200 BC-AD 200
Solid, hand-modeled, 1⅛ to 4¾ in.
These four figures come from different burials, where each once played a part in a narrative scene. Figures strapped to a pallet occur fairly often in West Coast ceramics, but their meaning is still a matter of speculation.

33
Mexico, Jalisco
Autlán region
Tuxcacuesco/Ortices style
100 BC-AD 300
Solid except seated female, hand-modeled
2¾ to 7¼ in.
A blend of West Coast styles, figures from this
region show a special effort to model the
planes of the face three-dimensionally, often
with defined cheekbones and chin. The blank
pellets used for eyes on the figure at far right
are even set into shallow eye sockets under a
brow ridge, and the nose of this figure is
particularly well observed and realistically
modeled. The relatively perfunctory treatment
of the bodies suggests the figures might even
have been intended as portraits.

34
Mexico, Jalisco
100 BC-AD 300
Solid, hand-modeled, 4⅝ to 6¾ in.
Small solid figures from Jalisco generally
display the same identifying characteristics as
better-known large hollow examples from this
area—exaggerated triangular noses, "coffee-
bean" eyes, and applied discs in the shoulder
area to indicate scarification welts. Aside from
a few decorative features, they're reduced,
like their Colima relatives (30-32), to features
necessary to place them in postures
appropriate to a genre scene.

35
Mexico, Jalisco
Teotihuacán influence
100 BC-AD 300
Solid, hand-modeled, 7½ in.
The simplified forms, smooth finish, and
symmetrically modeled facial features of this
figure give it a strength and monumentality
that belie its relatively small size. Although its
elongated face, prominent triangular nose,
and three-dimensional ears are typical Jalisco
traits, its stiff, frontal pose and leg posture
show influences from the more formalistic and
ceremonial culture of Teotihuacán (40c).

36
Mexico, Jalisco
Chinesco style
100 BC-AD 300
Hollow, hand-modeled, 6⅞ in.
The restrained simplicity of this figure
emphasizes the sculptural volume of its
repeated, swelling forms. The rows of shells
that adorn the outer edges of the ears are a
fashion common in West Coast Mexico.
Although figures from this area are generally
noted for awkward poses and distortions of
anatomy, this figure's refinement and the well-
observed naturalism of its squatting position
reflect a ceramic type that may represent a
divergent esthetic ideal.

37
Mexico, Nayarit
Chinesco style
100 BC-AD 300
Solid, hand-modeled, 3½ and 3 in.
These diminutive figures have been so
abstracted that they may seem like
caricatures of the human form. But the figure
on the left has considerable tactile appeal
precisely because of this simplification of its
well-proportioned and finely rounded volumes.
Its slightly more realistic companion here
achieves a pleasing visual rhythm through the
repetition of the heart-shaped lobes of its
coiffure in the arcs that define shoulders,
groin, feet, and buttocks.

38
Mexico, Nayarit
Ixtlán del Río type
100 BC-AD 300
Solid, hand-modeled, 10½ and 4½ in.
The anecdotal penchant common to the West
Coast cultures culminates in Nayarit models
of ballcourts, temples, and houses like this,
peopled with miniature figures in lively
activity. The sharply curved posture of the
separate squatting figure at right, with head
thrust forward and chin resting on his arms, is
seen often in small solid Nayarit figures. As in
many such figures, most details of clothing
and facial features are painted rather than
modeled.

39
Mexico, Distrito Federal
Early Teotihuacán style
Periods I and II
100 BC-AD 300
Solid, hand-modeled, 3⅛ to 5¼ in.
Village styles dominate early ceramic figures
from Teotihuacán, the ceremonial center of an
increasingly powerful theocratic city-state.
The fillets of clay used to indicate eyes and
mouth in period I figures accentuate the
pronounced tendency toward snoutlike faces.
The lavish attention paid to applied details of
clothing—capes, skirts, and a characteristic
wide headdress—suggests that the trappings
of ceremonial roles were already swallowing
up the unique qualities of the individual.

40
Mexico and Guatemala
Late Teotihuacán style
Periods III and IV
AD 300-650
Solid, hand-modeled and press-molded
2⅛ to 5½ in.
Press-mold figures like the two on the right
were produced throughout Middle America
during the height of Teotihuacán influence.
The pleasing arrangement of forms and
surface detail on the large standing figure
from Tiquisate, Guatemala, is enhanced by
bright colors added after firing, a typical
Teotihuacán feature. The articulated figure at
right, probably originally dressed in elaborate
textile regalia, shows the triangular face,
horizontal eye slits, and oversize ear discs
common to most Teotihuacán figures. With
their press-molded heads and hand-modeled
bodies, the two figures at left represent an
early stage in Teotihuacán mass-produced
ceramics.

41
Mexico, Michoacán
Las Delicias phase
Teotihuacán influence
AD 200-400
Solid, hand-modeled, 3½ and 3¾ in.
The low center of gravity, triangular face
shape, delineated knees, and closed leg-
stance of these small hand-modeled figures
recall regional village traditions (29).
Teotihuacán influence seems limited to their
snout-shaped faces (39) and narrow horizontal
eyes.

42
Mexico, Michoacán
Las Delicias phase
Teotihuacán influence
AD 200-400
Solid, hand-modeled, 7½ in.
The elegant simplicity and impassivity of this
large figure ally it to the Teotihuacán-
influenced example from Jalisco (35).
Although the fillet that outlines eyes and
mouth and the notch at the top of the head
may derive from Teotihuacán models, the
elongated torso and wide hips show
adherence to the local figural style (41).

43

Mexico, Oaxaca/Veracruz
Upper Papaloapan River

AD 200-500

Hollow, press-molded and hand-finished
6 to 8¼ in.

This troupe of "laughing" figures with arms
and legs outstretched in attitudes of
abandonment or exaltation may represent
ceremonial celebrants (and/or sacrificial
victims). The intertwined "scroll" designs with
which they are decorated are typical of the
elaborate, curvilinear surface ornamentation
that distinguishes Gulf Coast esthetics from
the more austere, sharp-angled, volumetric art
of central Mexico.

44

Mexico, Oaxaca
Zapotec culture
Monte Albán IIIa

AD 200-500

Hollow, hand-modeled, 6¼ and 4¾ in.

The great theocratic civilizations of the New
World increasingly stylized and abstracted
religious subject matter, as if to disguise its
meaning from the uninitiated. The symbolic
geometric elements of these small funerary
vessels identify the figures as the male and
female aspects of the Zapotec rain god Cocijo.
Their stiff, cross-legged, hands-on-knees pose
and the deep carving of their planes are
typical of Monte Albán ceramics of this period.

45
Mexico, Veracruz
Huastec culture
Panuco style
AD 100-300
Solid, hand-modeled, 5 to 11½ in.
Although the Huastec language belongs to the
Maya stock, Huasteca became geographically
isolated from major Maya centers and had
developed an independent cultural tradition
by the time these figures were made. Their flat
face planes and fully rounded torsos and limbs
are refined versions of a long local figural
tradition. The use of ribbons and pellets of
clay for decorative details continued until the
introduction of Teotihuacán-type molds. Even
the nose is separately modeled and
sometimes applied with enough pressure to
give the face a dished-out look.

46
Mexico, Campeche
Jaina Island
Maya culture
AD 600-900
Hollow, molded and hand-modeled
3¾ and 6½ in.
The kneeling figure at left is actually a small jar
whose detachable head is a stopper. The legs
and belly of the figure at right have been
exaggerated for its purpose as a rattle.
Although their forms have been simplified and
stylized, both figures have extraordinarily
realistic and expressive faces.

47
Mexico, Campeche
Jaina Island
Maya culture
AD 600-900
Solid, molded and hand-modeled
9¾ in.
The Maya potter's skillful command of the human figure sometimes misleads modern viewers to see a sculpture like this as a realistic portrait when it probably depicts a stylized, idealized type. Elite 8th and 9th century Maya practiced head elongation, scarification, and built-up nose bridges. This precisely sculpted figure represents both this ideal of beauty and an important, as yet unidentified, personage from Maya mythology.

48
Mexico, Campeche
Jaina Island
Maya culture
AD 600-900
Solid, molded and hand-modeled
5¼ to 8 in.
All these figures wear the thick, wide belt that identifies them as ballplayers. The two at right, which came from the same burial, may represent the mythical hero-twins who defeated the lords of the underworld in a symbolic ball game involving a series of trials that end in death and resurrection. The seated figure wearing an elaborate detachable headdress may also represent a mythological personage. There is no historical evidence that women ever played the Mayan ball game, although the apparently female figure at left is garbed as a participant.

49
Honduras, Ulúa Valley
Maya influence
AD 600-900
Hollow, press-molded, 3⅞ to 8 in.
These figures come from the southernmost frontier of Maya influence and are typical of the entirely mold-made figures in use for Maya burials shortly before the culture collapsed. Their postures suggest a degree of animation despite the compactness of their forms and the very shallow definition of their features and ornaments.

50
Mexico, Oaxaca/Veracruz
Isthmus of Tehuantepec
AD 900-1200
Solid, hand-modeled with press-mold faces
5¼ to 8¼ in.
Rarely do so many figures from the same burial remain together after they're unearthed. The gestures and costumes of this group suggest the figures are intended to enact some still undeciphered ceremony, though their original placement is unclear. The naturalistic treatment of the heavily lidded eyes, recurved noses, and open mouths of the mold-made heads recalls the figural styles of both Remojadas and Monte Albán (period II). The detachable face-mask/headdresses of the enthroned figure and the female figure at right conceal rudimentary head "stumps." The pillow is attached to the seated figure at left, but the throne is a separate piece.

51
Mexico, Distrito Federal
Toltec and Aztec cultures
AD 1100-1500
Hollow (l) and solid (r), mold-made
7¾ and 6¾ in.
These crudely molded figures are typical of those still being made at the time of the Spanish Conquest. According to early historical accounts, they depict deities, but recent scholarship suggests other interpretations.

Checklist of the Exhibition
(objects are identified by plate number alphabetically left to right)

1a. Gift of the Nova Albion Foundation. 1985.817
1b. Gift in memory of Natasha Congdon. 1979.39
1c-e. Anonymous loan. 19.1989, 22.1989, 21.1989

2a,c,d. Gift of the Nova Albion Foundation. 1985.745, 747, 744
2b. Anonymous gift. 1988.38

3a,c. Anonymous gift. 1988.40, 42
3b. Gift of Mr. & Mrs. Edward M. Strauss. 1984.52

4. Anonymous loan. 23.1989

5a,c. Gift of Mr. & Mrs. Wolfgang Pogzeba. 1970.290.2, 290.1
5b. Anonymous gift. 1988.39

6a-d. Gift of the Nova Albion Foundation. 1985.754, 758, 752, 1986.518

7a,b. Exchange. 1971.385.1-.2

8. Loan from Jan and Frederick R. Mayer. 495.1989

9. Gift of Mr. & Mrs. Cedric Marks. 1980.403

10a. Gift of Spencer Throckmorton. 1988.118
10b. Anonymous gift. 1988.37

11. Anonymous loan. 20.1989

12a-g. Gift of Mr. & Mrs. Harley Higbie and Mr. & Mrs. Frederick R. Mayer in honor of Masula and Harry Mannil. 1987.176, 179, 172, 162, 174, 161, 159

13a,b. Anonymous gift. 1988.150.2, 150.1
13c-i. Gift of Jan and Frederick R. Mayer. 1989.79.6, 79.3, 79.7, 79.4, 79.1, 79.2, 79.5

14a. Anonymous loan. 48.1989
14b. Gift of Fine Arts from Ancient Lands. 1988.114
14c,d. Gift in memory of Rafael Osona. 1988.128, 129
14e,f. Gift of Carolyn and Bill Stark. 1983.212, 213

15a,b. Gift of Fine Arts from Ancient Lands. 1989.80, 87

16. General acquisition funds. 1983.116

17a,e,g. Gift of James P. Economos. 1971.414, 376, 1972.247
17b. Gift of Mr. & Mrs. Jay C. Leff. 1981.34
17c. Marion Hendrie Fund. 1972.396
17d. Anonymous gift. 1977.176
17f,h. Gift of Carolyn and Bill Stark. 1983.210, 211

18a,b. Gift of Mr. & Mrs. Jay C. Leff. 1981.27, 32
18c. Gift of James P. Economos. 1973.235

19a. Gift of James P. Economos. 1972.159
19b. Gift of Carolyn and Bill Stark. 1983.209

20a,c. 1986 Collectors' Choice Benefit Fund. 1988.156, 157
20b,d. Anonymous gift. 1988.148, 149
20e. General acquisition funds. 1989.123

21a. Gift of Jan and Frederick R. Mayer. 1976.46
21b. Gift of Dr. M. Larry Ottis. 1987.512
21c. 1986 Collectors' Choice Benefit Fund. 1988.158

22. General acquisition funds. 1989.122

23a,b. Gift of Dr. M. Larry Ottis. 1987.514, 1984.601
23c. Gift of William R. Judy, Jr. 1987.219

24a,b. Anonymous gift. 1989.95, 1983.206
24c. Gift of Mr. & Mrs. Jay C. Leff. 1981.48

25a,b,e. Gift of Carolyn and Bill Stark. 1983.199, 204, 190
25c,d. General acquisition funds. 1974.230.2, 230.1

26a-d. Gift of Mr. & Mrs. Jay C. Leff. 1981.42, 1983.197, 1981.43, 41

27a,b. Gift of Mr. & Mrs. Edward Strauss. 1972.183.1-.2

28a. Gift of Cedric Marks. 1971.404
28b. Gift of James P. Economos. 1971.375

29a,d. Anonymous gift. 1989.57.1-.4, 1989.58.1-.4
29b. Gift of Margaret H. Margolin. 1986.676
29c,e. Bequest of Mrs. Bernham Hoyt. 1981.80, 78

29f. Gift of Mrs. Dolster Wetherill. 1970.296

30a,b. Gift of Mr. & Mrs. Alex Holland. 1965.200.2, 200.1

31a,b. Anonymous gift. 1971.343, 1989.96

32a,c,d. Gift of Margaret H. Margolin. 1986.686, 677, 691
32b. Funds from Mr. & Mrs. Frank Freyer and Mr. & Mrs. Ben Hall. 1983.112

33a,c. Anonymous gift. 1989.85, 86
33b. Gift of Judy Johnson. 1989.84

34a-d. Exchange. 1965.201.2, 201.1, 432, 433

35. Exchange. 1971.383

36. Gift of Carolyn and Bill Stark. 1981.372

37a,b. Funds from Walt Disney EPCOT Center. 1989.24, 25

38a. General acquisition funds. 1965.197
38b. Gift of Margaret H. Margolin. 1986.687

39a,d,f. Gift of Carolyn and Bill Stark. 1983.216, 215, 214
39b. Anonymous gift. 1988.140
39c. General acquisition funds. 1989.121
39e. Gift of the Goodrich Fund and anonymous donor. 1983.113

40a. Exchange. 1971.386
40b. Gift of Margaret H. Margolin. 1986.692
40c. Gift of Mr. & Mrs. Robert Pringle. 1985.400
40d. Anonymous gift. 1987.449

41a,b. Anonymous loan. 48.1974.2, 1

42. Anonymous gift. 1983.114

43a-d. Gift of William I. Lee. 1986.608, 607, 1985.637, 638

44a,b. Gift of James P. Economos. 1974.327, 328

45a. General acquisition funds. 1969.277
45b. Gift of William I. Lee. 1985.632
45c. Marion Hendrie Fund. 1972.399

46a. Funds from New World docents. 1988.141a,b
46b. Gift of William I. Lee. 1985.627

47. Gift in honor of Otto Bach. 1973.184

48a-d. Gift of William I. Lee. 1985.635, 1986.621, 622, 615

49a-c. Funds from an anonymous donor. 1988.153, 151, 152
49d. General acquisition funds, purchase in memory of John Ogle. 1989.73

50a-f. Anonymous gift. 1981.319.1-.6

51a. Gift of William I. Lee. 1986.611
51b. Gift of J. Anthony Falco. 1980.294